JUL 2 8 2009

W9-BRD-278

nature's
baby animals

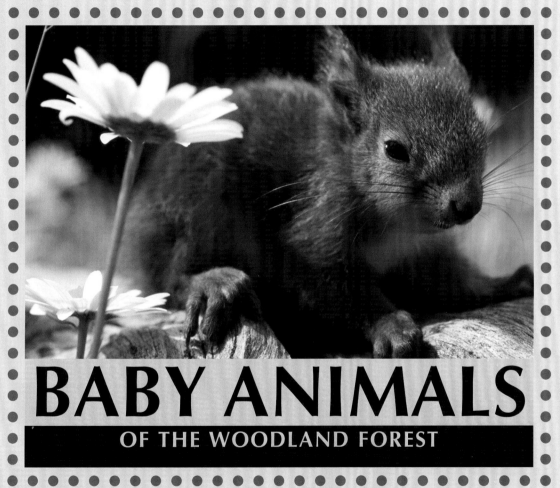

BABY ANIMALS
OF THE WOODLAND FOREST

Carmen Bredeson

Dennis L. Claussen, Ph.D., *Series Science Consultant* Professor of Zoology, Miami University, Oxford, Ohio

Allan A. De Fina, Ph.D., *Series Literacy Consultant* Past President of the New Jersey Reading Association, Chairperson, Department of Literacy Education, New Jersey City University, Jersey City, New Jersey

CONTENTS

ENDANGERED ANIMAL OF THE WOODLAND FOREST

WORDS TO KNOW

burrow [BUR oh]—A hole in the ground where some baby animals are born.

coyote [ky OH tee]—A kind of wild dog.

endangered [ehn DAYN jurd] **animal**—A kind of animal that is in danger of disappearing from the earth forever.

pouch [POWCH]—A sack-like part of some animals used to carry their babies.

WHERE ARE WOODLAND FORESTS?

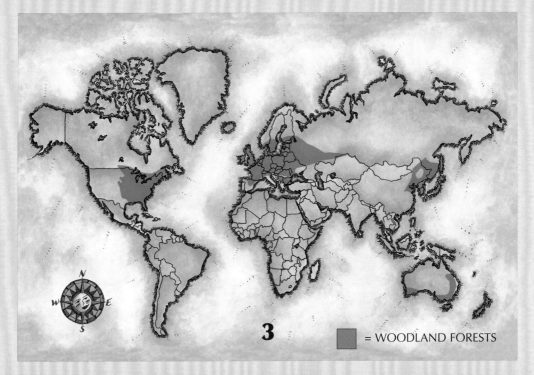

3

= WOODLAND FORESTS

WOODLAND FORESTS

Woodland forests are full of trees, bushes, and rivers. The weather is cold in the winter and warm in the summer. These forests are home to many kinds of animals.

5

BABY **OPOSSUM**

Baby opossums are tiny when they are born. They drink milk and grow in their mother's **pouch**. When they are bigger, the babies ride on their mother's back. She hunts for insects, nuts, and fruit for them to eat.

Black bear cubs are tiny when they are born in the winter. The cubs stay in a warm den with their mother. They drink their mother's milk and grow. When spring comes, the cubs leave the den for the first time.

BABY
BLACK BEAR

BABY **BALD EAGLE**

A bald eagle chick hatches from an egg. Its parents bring the chick meat and fish to eat. The chick flaps its wings to make them strong. When it is about two months old, the little eagle flies for the first time.

Baby red foxes are born in a warm **burrow**. When they are bigger, their mother teaches them to hunt for mice, beetles, fruit, and frogs. Foxes have very furry tails. They use them like blankets when nights are cold.

A baby fox is called a kit, cub, or pup.

BABY RED FOX

Five minutes old!

BABY **DEER**

A baby deer is called a fawn. It has spots on its fur for a few weeks. Spots help the fawn blend in with the plants and earth around it. This helps them stay safe from **coyotes** and wild dogs.

Red squirrels are born in a nest high in the trees. Their mother builds many nests. If there is danger from hawks or owls, she moves her babies to a new nest.

BABY
RED SQUIRREL

A baby bobcat is called a kitten.

BABY BOBCAT

Bobcat kittens are born in a cave or hollow tree. After a few weeks, their mother brings live mice to her kittens. They practice hunting with the mice. Soon the kittens are ready to go on a real hunt for food.

A baby panda is TINY and pink. The cub's black and white fur starts to grow in about a month. There are not many pandas left in the world. They have been hunted for their fur. Their forest homes in China have been cut down.

ENDANGERED
ANIMAL OF THE
WOODLAND FOREST

BABY
GIANT PANDA

Learn More

Books

Bishop, Nic. *Forest Explorer: A Life-Size Field Guide.* New York: Scholastic Press, 2004.

Crossingham, John, and Bobbie Kalman. *Endangered Pandas.* New York: Crabtree, 2005.

Lindeen, Carol K. *Life in a Forest.* Mankato, Minn.: Capstone Press, 2004.

Loughran, Donna. *Living in the Forest.* New York: Children's Press, 2004.

**Missouri Botanical Garden:
Biomes of the World.**
http://www.mbgnet.net
   Read about plants and animals of the biomes.

National Geographic Kids.
Creature Feature. "Giant Pandas."
http://kids.nationalgeographic.com/Animals/
CreatureFeature/Panda
   *Learn more about the giant
   panda through stories,
   photos, and videos.*

INDEX

~To our little Texans~Andrew, Charlie, and Kate~

Enslow Elementary, an imprint of Enslow Publishers, Inc.
Enslow Elementary® is a registered trademark of Enslow Publishers, Inc.

Copyright © 2009 by Carmen Bredeson

All rights reserved.

No part of this book may be reproduced by any means without the written permission of the publisher.

Library of Congress Cataloging-in-Publication Data

Bredeson, Carmen.
  Baby animals of the woodland forest / Carmen Bredeson.
    p. cm. — (Nature's baby animals)
  Summary: "Up-close photos and information about baby animals of the temperate forest biome"—Provided by publisher.
  Includes bibliographical references and index.
  ISBN-13: 978-0-7660-3005-3
  ISBN-10: 0-7660-3005-9
  1. Forest animals—Infancy—Juvenile literature. I. Title.
  QL112.B75 2009
  591.73—dc22
                          2007039470

Printed in the United States of America

10 9 8 7 6 5 4 3 2 1

Note to Parents and Teachers: The *Nature's Baby Animals* series supports the National Science Education Standards for K–4 science. The Words to Know section introduces subject-specific vocabulary words, including pronunciation and definitions. Early readers may need help with these new words.

To Our Readers: We have done our best to make sure all Internet Addresses in this book were active and appropriate when we went to press. However, the author and the publisher have no control over and assume no liability for the material available on those Internet sites or on other Web sites they may link to. Any comments or suggestions can be sent by e-mail to comments@enslow.com or to the address on the back cover.

Every effort has been made to locate all copyright holders of material used in this book. If any errors or omissions have occurred, corrections will be made in future editions of this book.

♻ Enslow Publishers, Inc., is committed to printing our books on recycled paper. The paper in every book contains 10% to 30% post-consumer waste (PCW). The cover board on the outside of each book contains 100% PCW. Our goal is to do our part to help young people and the environment too!

Photo Credits: Animals Animals: Dominique Braud, p. 11, Erwin & Peggy Bauer, p. 18, Gordon & Cathy Illg, p. 7; © Artville, LLC, p. 3; © David Ellis/Visuals Unlimited, pp. 2 (top), 10; © Keren Su/China Span/Alamy, pp. 2 (bottom), 21; Keren Su/China Span, p. 20; Minden Pictures: Gerry Ellis, p. 13, S & D & K Maslowski, p. 8, Sumio Harada, p. 16, Suzi Eszterhas, p. 9; naturepl.com: Bengt Lundberg, pp. 1, 17, T. J. Rich, p. 12; Photo Researchers, Inc.: Art Wolfe, p. 19; Shutterstock, pp. 5, 6, 14, 15, 23.

Cover Photo: Bengt Lundberg/naturepl.com

Enslow Elementary
an imprint of
Enslow Publishers, Inc.
40 Industrial Road
Box 398
Berkeley Heights, NJ 07922
USA
http://www.enslow.com